BUMPER
STICKERS
FOR THE
BRAIN

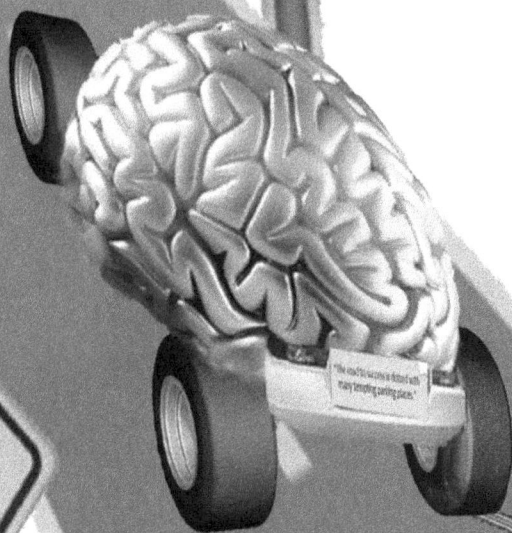

LEADERSHIP
QUOTES

SYLVIA LAFAIR

LEADERSHIP QUOTES: BUMPER STICKERS FOR THE BRAIN

By Sylvia Lafair, PhD

Creative Energy Options, Inc.
45 Country Place Lane
White Haven, PA 18661
570-636-3858
Email: info@ceoptions.com
www.ceoptions.com

creative energy options

CEO

PUBLISHING

Consider this book one filled with bumper stickers for the brain.

Often just a few words will jog your memory and open up new pathways of possibilities. Hearing a quote can give you a whole new perspective when you are stuck, looking for something fresh and new. It is good to lean on the poets and philosophers, the scientists and artists, the business people and educators to see through their eyes. It often will make you open your eyes much wider.

Quotes are meant to give us a tap on the shoulder, a kick in the rump, a hug from the heart. They are there to inspire, push us to action, and make us think about our beliefs, about what really matters.

Most quotes are short, a sentence or two and that is what makes them memorable. It takes a lot of discipline to say in a few words what most people say in paragraphs. Quotes are remembered because of their brevity and ability to get to the essence of a subject.

Quotes are elegant in the scientific meaning of the word. Elegant in science means taking the shortest route to get to what matters.

This book is, in that context, elegant. It is an easy book to follow. Most people simply open it to a page and let the quote speak to them. Others are searching for a specific point of view from a woman or a man, from either modern or ancient times and look at the name of the author before they even read the quote. Some are interested in the history of the person who is well known enough to be quoted and they want to know something about the human behind the words.

I put this together for all three needs.

It was actually fascinating to dig down and find out more about those whose names I knew yet were not real people till I began to dig into what made them tick, what made them come up with the very quote that has their name attached to it.

The quotes are meant to look at leadership and what lies at the core of all leaders: attitudes, beliefs, discipline, influence, emotion, vision, power, productivity and passion. Enjoy the sayings and learning about the flesh and blood of the people behind the words. Enjoy,

Sylvia Lafair, PhD

> **"Are parents really important? There is only one ticket to get to this planet and it comes from the two people who formed us."** --Sylvia Lafair

> **"What we learned in our original organization, the family, is what we bring to our present organization at work."**
> **--Sylvia Lafair**

> **"Until we transform patterns, productivity and creativity are diminished."**
> **--Sylvia Lafair**

"Our families do not intentionally set out to put us in little boxes, yet somehow we end up in them, unless we stay observant."

--Sylvia Lafair

"Are we meant to be picture perfect women? To airbrush or not to airbrush, you decide." --Sylvia Lafair

"It will take GUTSY women and BOLD men to help make lasting positive change happen." -- Sylvia Lafair

"It is the combination of logic and intuition that gives life rich meaning and depth."

--Sylvia Lafair

"It is a GUTSY act to speak the unspeakable."

--Sylvia Lafair

> "I'm not offended by all the dumb blond jokes because I know I'm not dumb. I also know I'm not blond."
>
> -- Dolly Parton

Dolly Parton, known for her singing and acting is an icon for authenticity. Her talents span many fields and one area that is often not as well-known is in her philanthropic endeavors. In 1996, Dolly launched the "Imagination Library" to benefit the children of her home town of Sevierville, Tennessee. She wanted youngsters to be excited about reading and wanted every child to have books, regardless of their family's income. They were specially selected books sent to all children born in the town, one every month. By 2000 she said she would make the program available to any community willing to partner with her to support the effort locally. Over 1600 communities around the world now support almost 700,000 children each month.

Statistics indicate that this simple, yet powerful effort that Dolly started improves early childhood literacy and here's how you can get involved.

Go to www.imaginationlibrary.com and help make the world just that much better, one book, one caring action at a time.

"Simplicity is the ultimate sophistication."
-- Leonardo da Vinci

"Don't talk unless you can improve the
silence."

-- Ritu Ghatourey

"Courage is what it takes to stand up and
speak; Courage is also what it takes to sit
down and listen."
-- Winston Churchill

"Freedom is actually a bigger game than
power. Power is about what you can con-
trol. Freedom is about what you can
unleash."
-- Harriet Rubin

"Even before we were born gender stereotypes influenced our behavior and how we will respond to life." --Sylvia Lafair

"What forms who we will become is family, culture, and crises."

--Sylvia Lafair

"Does being polite mean never saying what you really think?"

--Sylvia Lafair

"Our decisions as females are shaped by culture as well as biology; it is time to question why we behave the way we do and change what no longer works."

--Sylvia Lafair

"During times of accelerated change the pendulum goes to extremes before it finds the middle ground."

--Sylvia Lafair

"Do not allow people to dim your shine because they are blinded. Tell them to put on some sunglasses, cuz we were born this way bitch!"

-- Lady Gaga

"Example is not the main thing in influencing others, it's the only thing."

-- Dr. Albert Schweitzer

"Beneath the makeup and behind the smile I am just a girl who wishes for the world."

-- Marilyn Monroe

"I am doing that which I cannot do in order that I may learn how to do it."

-- Pablo Picasso

"When we are alert to why certain people and situations push our buttons, we are then in charge of the best ways to react."

--Sylvia Lafair

"Our stories are both personal and universal, and in sharing them we help each other grow."

--Sylvia Lafair

"Tears are the part of us that was frozen and beginning to defrost."

--Sylvia Lafair

"Once we can observe a pattern that we repeat and repeat, it no longer has power over us."

--Sylvia Lafair

"Sometimes thinking you are the opposite is just being stuck at the other end of the same continuum."

--Sylvia Lafair

> **Change your thoughts and you change the world.**
>
> **--Harold R. McAlindon, Former President of the Board at Cambridge Philosophy Institute**

A woman pulled into a gas station on the outskirts of town. As she filled her tank, she remarked to the owner, "I've just accepted a job in town here. I've never been to this part of the country before...what are people like here?"

"What are people like where you came from?" the owner asked.

"Not so nice," the woman replied. "In fact, they could be quite rude."

The owner shook his head. "Well, I'm afraid you'll find the people in this town to be the same way."

Just then another car pulled into the station. "Excuse me," the driver called out. "I'm just moving to this area. Is it nice here?"

"Was it nice where you came from?" the owner inquired.

"Oh, yes! I came from a great place. The people were friendly, and I hated to leave."

"Well, you'll find the same to be true of this town.

"Thanks!" yelled the driver as he pulled away.

"So what is this town really like?" asked the woman, now irritated with the owner's conflicting reports.

The owner just shrugged his shoulders. "It's all a matter of perception. You'll find things to be just the way you think they are."

Adapted from the Positive Christianity Web Site

"Nothing is a waste of time if you use the experience wisely."
                    -- Auguste Rodin

"When choosing between two evils, I always like to do the one I've never tried before."
                    -- Mae West

"We either make ourselves or we make ourselves strong. The amount of miserable work is the same."
                    -- Carlos Castaneda

"Luck is what happens when preparation meets opportunity."
                    -- Seneca (Roman Philosopher)

"You may think that negative invisible roles and patterns are only in *dysfunctional families*, yet they are in every one of us."

--Sylvia Lafair

"Men love to use the word *powerful* to describe themselves, while words for women in power are much more colorful."

--Sylvia Lafair

"Every mother/daughter relationship stands on the shoulders of all the women who came before."

--Sylvia Lafair

"Telling the truth is a disciplined high level art form few have mastered."

--Sylvia Lafair

"We are born from a relationship, through a relationship, into a relationship. We are all connected by relationship and that is what makes the world go round." --Sylvia Lafair

"We are all faced with a series of great opportunities brilliantly disguised as impossible situations."
-- Charles Swindoll

"Mistakes are part of the dues one pays for a full life."
-- Sophia Loren

"Admit your errors before someone else exaggerates them."
-- Andrew Mason

"Both optimists and pessimists contribute to our society. The optimist invents the airplane; and the pessimist, the parachute."
-- Gil Stern

"The answer is always in the entire story, not just in a piece of it."

--Sylvia Lafair

"Telling the truth is NOT the same as spilling your guts."

--Sylvia Lafair

"Talking with our parents in a more honest and open way can change the way we talk with our boss and direct reports at work." --Sylvia Lafair

"You cannot initially see your own annoying patterns that remain invisible; always easier to see what is wrong with someone else." --Sylvia Lafair

"The freedom that comes from knowing your history gives you power over the choices you make moving forward."

--Sylvia Lafair

> "Problems are only opportunities with thorns on them."
> -- Hugh Miller ("Snow on the Wind")

> "Behold the turtle.
> He makes great progress only when he sticks his neck out."
> -- James B. Conant

James Bryant Conant, a chemist turned educator, made some bold moves that made a difference. In 1933, when he became President of Harvard University, he abolished athletic scholarships and instituted an *up or out* policy under which students who were not promoted were terminated.

He adopted co-educational classes and led the cause to have women admitted to Harvard Medical and Law Schools for the first time. He took chances to *stick his neck out* as his quote indicates.

After his death a sealed brown manila envelope was handed to the first president in the 21st Century. It contained a letter in which Conant expressed his hopes and fears for future successors. He wrote it many years before, and his hope was *that Harvard will maintain the traditions of academic freedom and of tolerance* of those 70 years earlier.

"*Drama Queens* and *Kings* flood the workplace with emotions that make it impossible to get work done. Lots of adrenaline that is like an energy addiction."   --Sylvia Lafair

"*Martyrs* are procrastinators at the other end of the scale. They do everyone's work so they can be seen as "over busy" and thus won't be called on the carpet for their own mediocre work."   --Sylvia Lafair

"*Pleasers* cannot set limits and say *yes* to everything, so truth is unknown and they do not offer opinions. They want to fit in rather than do anything original or creative."
                    --Sylvia Lafair

"*Avoiders* abound at work when there is conflict brewing, and they may be seen as vulnerable. Better to leave the situation and their mantra is *better safe than sorry*."

                    --Sylvia Lafair

"*Deniers* at work are the ones with the rose-colored glasses and just do NOT SEE what is right in front of them. They are the main ones who hold up innovation and love the status quo."   --Sylvia Lafair

"The best way to get people to think out of the box is not to create the box in the first place."
-- Martin Cooper

"The great leaders are like the best conductors; they reach beyond the notes to reach the magic in the players."
-- Blaine Lee

"When spider webs unite they can tie up a lion."
-- Ethiopian Proverb

"Individuals play the game, but teams beat the odds."
-- SEAL team saying

"There is always a sense of dissatisfaction or lack of completion until the puzzle pieces of our lives are put in place."

--Sylvia Lafair

"Females often get hooked into being pleasers especially when we become aware it's important to be part of an *in crowd.*"

--Sylvia Lafair

"The old days of padded shoulders in business suits did not make us powerful, only absurd."

--Sylvia Lafair

"For males and females it is time to consider *her story* as we continue to look at *history.*"

--Sylvia Lafair

"We can all live successfully for one day. Achieving high purpose means making that the pattern for every day."

--Sylvia Lafair

> "A group becomes a team when each member is sure enough of himself and his contribution to praise the skills of the others."
> -- Norman Shilde

A Story to help YOU pay ATTENTION

During my second month of nursing school, our professor gave us a pop quiz.

I was a conscientious student and had breezed through the questions, until I read the last one: *"What is the first name of the woman who cleans the school?"* Surely this was some kind of joke. I had seen the cleaning woman several times. She was tall, dark-haired and in her 50's, but how would I know her name?

I handed in my paper, leaving the last question blank.

Before class ended, one student asked if the last question would count toward our quiz grade.

"Absolutely," said the professor. *"In your careers you will meet many people. All are significant."*

I've never forgotten that lesson. I also learned that her name was Dorothy.

--Anonymous

> "My grandfather once told me that there were two kinds of people: those who do the work and those who take the credit. He told me to try to be in the first group, there was much less competition."
> -- Indira Gandhi (Prime Minister of India)

> "It is not the strongest of the species that survive nor the most intelligent, but the one most responsive to change."
> -- Charles Darwin

> "I suppose leadership at one time meant muscles; but today it means getting along with people."
> -- Mohandas Gandhi

> "The growth and development of people is the highest calling of leadership."
> -- Harvey Firestone

"Action is key in any situation, and interaction is even more to the point."

--Sylvia Lafair

"When you fall into the judgment trap you are already prepared for a fight that will have an ugly ending."   --Sylvia Lafair

"Companies that offer opportunities for self-awareness programs have an edge in retaining the best and brightest employees."   --Sylvia Lafair

"PatternAware™ Leadership Programs are for the 'A' team including authenticity, accountability, accuracy, action and achievement."   --Sylvia Lafair

"Business decisions are too often made behind closed doors before meetings even start."   --Sylvia Lafair

"Management is doing things right;
leadership is doing the right thing."
                            -- Peter Drucker

"The only thing that doesn't abide by
majority rule is a person's conscience."
                            -- Harper Lee

"If your actions inspire others to dream
more, learn more, do more and become
more, you are a leader."
-- John Quincy Adams (6th U.S. President)

"There are no traffic jams along the extra
mile."
                            -- Roger Staubach

"Most business leaders are not trained to think systemically, but in dichotomies so that when problems occur there is a predictable analytic response of sort and judge."   --Sylvia Lafair

"In business real, meaningful and profitable change is possible only if we start to see work teams not as disconnected parts but as living organisms at are unique and complex."
--Sylvia Lafair

"There is a sad situation that often occurs when outdated family patterns we never addressed as we grew up flare up constantly and automatically in our professional lives."
--Sylvia Lafair

"When we grow into adulthood we layer a new web of relationships – those of our work team – on top of the original family system."   --Sylvia Lafair

"Families and work groups are structurally similar, and the day-to-day workings of both groups are fundamentally the same."
--Sylvia Lafair

> "When everyone is thinking the same, no one is thinking."
>
> -- John Wooden

John Wooden was ranked by ESPN as the greatest coach of all times, across all sports. He led UCLA to record wins still unmatched in the world of basketball. His players, including legends such as Bill Walton and Kareem Abdul-Jabbar, were like extended family and he emphasized that winning was more than scoring.

Wooden's 7 point creed was given to him by his father Joshua upon his graduation from grammar school. He took this legacy and brought a deep sense of sports as a playing field for learning about life.

Here are the 7 points. Copy and give to a sixth grader.

- Be true to yourself
- Make each day your masterpiece
- Help others
- Drink deeply from good books
- Make friendship a fine art
- Build a shelter against a rainy day
- Pray for guidance and give thanks for your blessings every day

"Fate has a way of stepping in when we have run out of ideas or options, so pay attention."

--Sylvia Lafair

"Our culture has a tendency to be addicted to the negative and it will take all of us to say *no* to all the things that do not work and focus on what is working."   --Sylvia Lafair

"Being both soft and strong, being both daring and caring is the work of 21st Century women and men."

--Sylvia Lafair

"A big question for working mothers and fathers is: what is the difference between child care and caring for children?"

--Sylvia Lafair

"It takes lots of *NOTS* to *KNOT* our emotions."

--Sylvia Lafair

"You have brains in your head you have feet in your shoes,
you can steer yourself any direction you choose."
-- Dr. Seuss

"Leadership and learning are indispensable to each other."
-- John F. Kennedy

"When you feel grateful, you become great and eventually attract great things."
-- Plato

It is in the nature of man to rise to greatness if greatness is expected of him."
-- John Steinbeck

"Leadership is about claiming and taming the world of interpersonal relationships."

--Sylvia Lafair

"When we break the cycle of pattern repetition and discard our burdensome family baggage it is replaced with renewed creative energy at work and at home."   --Sylvia Lafair

"Although we cannot make up for lost years, when truths surface, we can gain a new perspective and often that is the key to viewing all situations from a different lens."

--Sylvia Lafair

"Changing behavior in anything beyond a superficial way requires discipline, time and commitment. Instant change is simply a marketing ploy and never works."--Sylvia Lafair

"The blame game gets us nowhere. It takes effort to transcend blame and review and analyze the whole system where real change is waiting to be found."   --Sylvia Lafair

"Enthusiasm is the mother of effort, and
without it nothing great was ever
achieved."
-- Ralph Waldo Emerson

"The road to success is dotted with many
tempting parking places."
-- Author unknown

"Strong people don't follow the crowd
even when the crowd is against them."
--Sonya Parker

"If you want to build a ship, don't
drum up people to gather
wood, divide the work, and give
orders. Instead teach them
to yearn for the vast and endless sea."
-- Antoine de Saint-Exupery

> "That's all a man can hope for during his lifetime - to set an example - and when he is dead, to be an inspiration for history."
> --President, William McKinley

William McKinley, the 25th President of the United States, once had to choose between two equally qualified men for a key job. He puzzled over the choice until he remembered a long-ago incident.

On a rainy night, McKinley had boarded a crowded streetcar. Once of the men he was now considering had also been aboard, though he didn't see McKinley. Then an old woman carrying a basket of laundry struggled into the car, looking in vain for a seat. The job candidate pretended not to see her and kept his seat. McKinlwy gave up his seat to help her out.

Remembering the episode, which he called "this little omission of kindness," McKinley decided against the man on the streetcar. Our decisions – even the small, fleeting ones – tell a lot about us.

Only you can be yourself. No one else is qualified the for the job.

Adapted from *Presidential Anecdotes*
Paul F. Boller, Jr. Penguin Books

"Telling *Heart Truth* is just about the same as telling *Hard Truth*, no matter what, it's the better way to go."

--Sylvia Lafair

"It's never just about the project at work; it's always about relationships."

--Sylvia Lafair

"The only way OUT of difficulties is to Observe, Understand and Transform and then the magic happens."

--Sylvia Lafair

"Women today can no longer be shushed or denied. They are standing on the shoulders of the past to be heard and make a difference." --Sylvia Lafair

"Hidden behavior patterns wreak havoc in the workplace in the form of power games, *cover your butt* strategies, and a variety of disruptive office politics." --Sylvia Lafair

"If in the last few years you haven't discarded a major opinion or acquired a new one, check your pulse. You may be dead."
-- Gelett Burgess

"When you are finished changing, you are finished."
-- Benjamin Franklin

"There is only one real sin and that is to persuade oneself that the second-best is anything but second best."
-- Doris Lessing

"The first problem for all of us, men and women, is not to learn but to unlearn."
-- Gloria Steinem

"We have been trained to talk *at* people, rather than engage in an honest dialogue that we think will leave us feeling defenseless and naked."   --Sylvia Lafair

"Transforming a team dynamic takes time and is worth the effort in which individuals learn to communicate the truth and elevate relationships to a whole new level."

--Sylvia Lafair

"Residing on the edges of our consciousness invisible patterns torture us, like an annoying itch we cannot seem to scratch. Until we learn the way OUT to observe, understand, and transform."   --Sylvia Lafair

"Unresolved family patterns lead to thwarted careers, strained personal relationships, and physical and emotional upset."   --Sylvia Lafair

"The vast majority of 21st Century work places are rife with negativity, tension a dissatisfied employees who do the minimum to get their paycheck."   --Sylvia Lafair

"When one tugs at a single thing in nature, he finds it attached to the rest of the world."

--John Muir (1838-1914) Naturalist, Author

"An invisible red thread connects those who are destined to meet, regardless of time, place, or circumstance. The thread may stretch or tangle, but will never break."

--Chinese Proverb

"All great literature is one of two stories; a man goes on a journey or a stranger comes to town."

-- Leo Tolstoy

"All the world's a stage and most of us are just unrehearsed."

--From the Motion Picture, *Young Cassidy*

"For what is done or learned by one class of women becomes the property of all women."
-- Elizabeth Blackwell

"Coming together is a beginning; keeping together is progress; working together is success."
-- Henry Ford

"Nothing so conclusively proves a man's ability to lead others as what he does from day to day to lead himself."
-- Thomas J. Watson

"Treat a man as he is and he will remain as he is. Treat a man as he can be and he will become as he can and should be."
-- Johann Wolfgang von Goethe

"You can have *ex-bosses, ex- direct reports, even ex- spouses*, but we cannot have an *ex-mother*, just one you don't see, or an *ex-father* you steer clear of."   --Sylvia Lafair

"How often do we talk about *taking refuge* at home when problems break and work becomes stressful, and *losing ourselves in our work* when problems break out at home."

--Sylvia Lafair

"Our tendency to want to solve problems quickly, is partially driven by our need to alleviate anxiety."

--Sylvia Lafair

"All change management processes go through a period called 'the ugly middle' when it looks impossible for anything positive to happen."

--Sylvia Lafair

"Splitters, the most divisive in the workplace, talk out of both sides of their mouths and love to stir up conflict. They are masters of covert power games that destroy team productivity."

--Sylvia Lafair

> **"My job is not to be easy on people. My job is to make them better."**
>
> **--Steve Jobs**

Steve Jobs was not your typical Silicon Valley CEO. Unlike most tech companies founders, he had neither any engineering experience nor any business training. After all, he dropped out of college after one semester! Few people know that Steve Jobs was never CEO of Apple in his first run there: the company was run by older executives and investors, and Steve Jobs actually helped them hire an experienced, 'well-rounded' CEO in 1983, John Sculley. However, Jobs was kicked out of Apple by Sculley two years later and he watched him bring the company to naught during his tenure.

The lesson he learned from this painful experience was to trust his own beliefs and values, and completely disregard the conventional views on how to run a company, including the traditional duties of a CEO. He delegated those duties to members of his executive team, most notably his second-in-command and eventual successor, Tim Cook, and focused on what he was best at: creating products, recruiting, marketing, and of course, being the public face of the company. He described it in a 2004 interview: *"I get to spend my time on the forward-looking stuff. My top executives take half the other work off my plate. They love it, and I love it."*

From http://allaboutstevejobs.com/persona/steveatwork.php

"Becoming a leader is synonymous with becoming yourself; it is precisely that simple, and it is also that difficult."
-- Warren Bennis

"Leadership is NOT about changing the mindset of the individual or group, but in the cultivation of an environment that brings out the best and even inspires the individuals in that group to do what needs to be done."
-- Arthur Carmazzi

"Snowflakes are one of nature's most fragile things, but just look at what they can do when they stick together."
-- Anonymous

Tell me and I'll forget; show me and I may remember; involve me and I'll understand."
-- Chinese proverb

"Conflict runs rampant in the workplace because of our natural and universal tendency to bring our *internal families* to work with us."
                                                    --Sylvia Lafair

"Experiences from childhood are still alive in new situations at work, where we still have unconscious expectations of how people we meet are supposed to look, sound, and act."
                                                    --Sylvia Lafair

"Standard interventions in workplace conflict stay on superficial, symptomatic levels often putting blame on one person hoping with finer pointing and disciplinary actions all will be fine."   --Sylvia Lafair

"Super achievers in the workplace are conditioned to defend, explain and justify why their way works best. This behavior breeds fear and resentment and limits ability for teams to trust."   --Sylvia Lafair

"Rebels are work are an HR nightmare. They thrive on negative attention and want change to happen at an unrealistic rate just to suit their needs."
                                                    --Sylvia Lafair

"If we all did things we are capable of
doing we would literally astound
ourselves."
-- Thomas Edison

"You grow up the day you have your first
real laugh at yourself."
-- Ethel Barrymore

"Twenty years from now you will be more
disappointed by the things you didn't do
than by the ones you did do."
-- Mark Twain

"Help one another, is part of the religion
of sisterhood."
-- Louisa May Alcott

The book, *Little Women* is a classic that is often handed down from generation to generation. The quotes and some of the language may seem dated in today's fast-paced world. Yet, the eternal truths of living, loving, family, community and nation are really much the same as they were during the time of the Civil War.

Louisa was the second oldest of four sisters and her world-famous book is modeled after her family life. Louisa was raised in a non-traditional way by her parents, her father being a transcendentalist educator. Today the group that was filled with intellectuals and people who saw a new way to live would be labeled *hippies*.

Her early education included lessons from naturalist Henry David Thoreau as well as studies with Ralph Waldo Emerson, Nathaniel Hawthorne and Margaret Fuller who were all family friends.

While she never married, as did her sisters, when her youngest sister died from childbirth fever she took her niece and raised her as her own.

Alcott was a strong willed woman and the character of Jo in "Little Women" is modeled after her own willingness to speak out and be heard. The family was a perfect place for learning to be strong and unafraid. Alcott was an abolitionist and her family served as station masters on the Underground Railroad.

She would have been a perfect fit in the 1960's and can be imagined singing *Give Peace a Chance*. Her work is what we call *evergreen* and will stay young and fresh generation after generation. She was known to say that she believed it is as much a right and duty for women to do something with their lives and should not be satisfied with the frivolous parts that men wanted to give to women.

"Procrastinators fail to follow through and then become indignant when held responsible claiming they were never given the right information or tolls to work with."

                                        --Sylvia Lafair

"The office clown loves to divert situations in which they are uncomfortable so they can hide their underlying vulnerability."

                                        --Sylvia Lafair

"Persecutors, aka bullies, need to feel important, dominate conversations, and demand to be the center of attention. They make sure that others are proven wrong over and over."   --Sylvia Lafair

"Victims at work are the consummate complainers who feel inadequate and are not able to take the bull by the horns to do something in a different way. They thrive on being rescued."   --Sylvia Lafair

"Rescuers LOVE to save victims by solving their problems and then making sure they are seen as heroes. This is self-serving altruism so rescuers don't have to look at their own inadequacies."   --Sylvia Lafair

"The difference between try and triumph
is a little umph."
-- Anonymous

"Whoever said money can't buy happiness
didn't know where to shop."
-- Gertrude Stein

"Some say our national pastime is
baseball. Not me; it's gossip."
-- Erma Bombeck

"A group of idiots led by a wise woman
can defeat a group of wise people led by an
idiot."
-- Senora Roy

"We are all different. Even better, we are all UNIQUE."
> --Sylvia Lafair

"Those who remain silent about abuses from the past are guilty too."
> --Sylvia Lafair

"It is dangerous and costly for self-awareness and leadership development to be separated."
> --Sylvia Lafair

"Sometimes the most important part of a conversation comes in the last three minutes."
> --Sylvia Lafair

"Opening up the locked closets where truth often resides is risky and liberating."
> --Sylvia Lafair

> **The truth is that there is nothing noble in being superior to somebody else. The only real nobility is in being superior to your former self.**
>
> **--Whitney Young, Civil Rights Leader (1921-1971)**

"Whitney understood power, he understood politics, and most of all he understood people. They said Martin was in the streets, Roy and Thurgood were in the courts, and Whitney was in the boardroom. One could not have been successful without the other."

- Vernon Jordan, CEO National Urban League

One of the most celebrated leaders of the Civil Rights era, Whitney Young helped thousands of people struggling against discrimination by taking the fight directly to those in power. However, because those in power were the same white elite that he shook hands, made deals, and worked with behind the scenes, he was also one of the most controversial figures in the Civil Rights movement and viewed by some as an "Uncle Tom." Follow the story of Young's journey from the segregated South to national campaign for equal rights as his legacy of pragmatism and deliberative negotiation resonates in today's political climate.

http://www.pbs.org/independentlens/powerbroker/

"Staff meetings have all the emotional elements of a family gathering and it is important to be a great orchestra leader to keep things moving forward and not derailing."   --Sylvia Lafair

"Taking on the role of change agent is not for the faint of heart. You have to be a risk taker for real and lasting change to happen."

--Sylvia Lafair

"Dialogue is an art form that all leaders must learn. It goes past right and wrong to question what really matters and then making decisions."   --Sylvia Lafair

"Work is NOT a rehab facility and yet, we need to help employees grow and flourish."

--Sylvia Lafair

"The search for truth and meaning is foundational for all teams. Finding new ways to see, hear and experience each other is what sets a team free for creative and productive work."   --Sylvia Lafair

A man was lost while driving through the countryside. As he tried to read a map, he accidently drove off the road into a ditch. Though he wasn't injured, his car was stuck deep in the mud. So the man walked to a nearby farm to ask for help.

"Ole Pal can get you out of that ditch," said the farmer, pointing to an old mule standing in a field. The man looked at the haggardly mule and looked at the farmer who just stood there repeating, "Yep, Ole Pal can do the job." The man figured he had nothing to lose. The two men and Ole Pal made their way back to the ditch.

The farmer hitched the mule to the car. With a snap of the reins he shouted, "Pull, Fritz! Pull, Tom! Pull, Ole Pal!" And the mule pulled the car from the ditch with very little effort.

The man was amazed. He thanked the farmer, patted the mule and asked, "Why did you call out all of those other names before you called Ole Pal?"

The farmer grinned and said, "Ole Pal is just about blind. As long as he believes he's part of a team, he doesn't mind pulling."

Adapted from Some Folks Feel the Rain...Others Just Get Wet
– James W. Moore, Dimensions

"Being authentic means taking ownership of the tensions and complexities that exist in the workplace, asking questions to gain clarity, and telling the truth without blame or judgment."   --Sylvia Lafair

"Our responsibility is to decide which patterns from the past serve us and release the rest."

--Sylvia Lafair

"We talk about work-life balance as if work and life were chunks of matter on opposite sides of a balance scale."

--Sylvia Lafair

"Often we don't reveal much about our private lives to our colleagues and do not mention our work challenges to our spouses or partners."   --Sylvia Lafair

"The search for truth and meaning is foundational for all teams. Finding new ways to see, hear and experience each other is what sets a team free for creative and productive work."   --Sylvia Lafair

Sylvia Lafair, PhD has dedicated her career to helping individuals become their best. First as a psychologist working with families and couples and then making a left hand turn into the world of business leadership and team development.

Her "UNIQUE" ideas have had widespread influence in corporations, family firms, and entrepreneurial start-ups.

The past 25 years have been spent helping executives, managers, and teams connect the dots of how personal and professional behavior cannot be separated. She has trained a staff of executive coaches and facilitators in her Pattern Aware™ model.

What has been eye-opening in all manner of organizations is that when stress hits the hot button we all tend to revert to patterns from childhood that were there to keep us safe. While they may have helped at five or seven or twelve, they can run havoc in adult relationships.

Working with companies around the world it became clear that the universal aspects of what it means to be in relationships is not very different regardless of culture, size of company, or product. Everywhere there is the yearning for all of us to get along. Dr. Lafair's innovative work gives us the directives to make this happen.

Her book 'Don't Bring It to Work' has won nine awards and with its companion 'Pattern Aware Success Guide,' has been used in graduate programs and by work teams worldwide.

Her book, 'GUTSY: How Women Leaders Make Change' has also won six book awards and led to her highly successful **GUTSY Women Weekend Retreats**.

This newest book *'UNIQUE: How Story Sparks Diversity, Inclusion and Engagement,'* is based on the powerful model of storytelling called **Sankofa Mapping ™**.

Dr. Lafair's abilities to blend story with fact and humor make her a sought after speaker, workshop facilitator, and executive coach.

Her **Total Leadership Connections Program ™**, now in its fifteenth year, has been named one of the top leadership development programs in 2015 by Leadership Excellence/H.R.com, making this the third year in a row.

Dr. Lafair has been featured in *The Wall Street Journal, Forbes* and *Time* as well as on the *Today Show* with Kathie Lee and Hoda.

For further information or to book Dr. Lafair for a consultation or speaking engagement please call her office at 570.636.3858 or email her directly at sylvia@ceoptions.com.